D0021211

a gift for you as you graduate

Anar

TO

Sonua

FROM

2003 April 06

DATE

Prayers
AND
Promises
FOR THE
Graduate

G. A. Myers

HOWARD
PUBLISHING CO.

Our purpose at Howard Publishing is to:

- *Increase faith* in the hearts of growing Christians
- *Inspire holiness* in the lives of believers
- *Instill hope* in the hearts of struggling people everywhere

Because He's coming again!

Prayers and Promises for the Graduate © 2003 by G. A. Myers
All rights reserved. Printed in the United States of America
Published by Howard Publishing Co., Inc.
3117 North 7th Street, West Monroe, LA 71291-2227

03   04   05   06   07   08   09   10   11   12   10   9   8   7   6   5   4   3   2   1

Edited by Between the Lines
Cover design by LinDee Loveland
Interior design by Stephanie Denney

Library of Congress Cataloging-in-Publication Data

Myers, G. A., 1955-
    Prayers and promises for the graduate / G.A. Myers.
       p. cm.
    ISBN 1-58229-299-X
      1. Youth—Prayer-books and devotions—English. 2. College graduates—Prayer-books and
devotions—English. 3. High school graduates—Prayer-books and devotions—English. I.
Title.

BV283. Y6 M94 2003
242'.634—dc21

                                                                    2002038887

Scripture taken from the HOLY BIBLE, NEW INTERNATIONAL VERSION®. Copyright ©
1973, 1978, 1984 International Bible Society. Used by permission of Zondervan Publishing
House. All rights reserved.

Contents

Be not forgetful of prayer.
Every time you pray,
if your prayer is sincere,
there will be new feeling and
new meaning in it,
which will give you courage,
and you will understand
that prayer is an education.

FYODOR DOSTOYEVSKI

FYODOR
DOSTOYEVSKI

A Word to the Reader

Graduation is a special time. It's the culmination of years of hard work and determination, of struggles and triumphs. Finally, you've made it. It's a time of excitement, of looking forward to the future and all it holds in store for you. It's also a time of transition, and that means you'll be facing new challenges. Though you've learned a great deal already, your daily steps now will call for a new kind of wisdom, a deeper strength to make your dreams reality. Throughout your education, you've benefited from the wisdom of teachers and the guidance of advisors. But now, your questions are bigger—more important—because they're about your life and the path you will take. Where do you turn for that kind of guidance?

Prayers and Promises for the Graduate is a unique book filled with prayers from someone like you and answers from the best Advisor you'll ever have—your heavenly Father.

You'll quickly identify with the prayers, written as letters to a loving God, because they convey the needs, emotions, feelings, and struggles you face as you graduate and start the next phase of your life. In heaven's response, you'll read personalized, paraphrased scriptures—God's promises—also written as letters; and you'll experience the encouraging, assuring presence and loving warmth only heaven can give.

The promises that fill these heavenly letters will remain with you, inspire you, and fill you with hope. Let this little book bring you closer to heaven and to the promises that will impact your todays, tomorrows, and the rest of your life.

A Graduate's Prayer

Dear Father,

It's Your child again, needing You as always. I'm writing about something I need help with but am ashamed to admit—especially to You whose fearlessness is legendary and whose steps have never known retreat. Though I'm excited about graduating, I'm also afraid. Maybe it's the uncertainty of the future or even my failures of the past. It could be the deeper sense of responsibility I'm feeling toward friends and family. I'm apprehensive about letting down those I love most. You see, they have expectations of me that I'm not sure I can live up to. I'm fearful I won't meet my own expectations, much less those of others.

I've heard the stories of how You have led the charge in situations that others considered a lost cause, how You have strengthened the legs of the timid and given honor and promise to those who cowered in fear.

I don't want to be afraid. I want to live a courageous life, but I need to hear from You. Only Your words of courage and confidence will strengthen my resolve for the challenges that lie ahead.

Your Child Who Needs Courage

A Heavenly Promise

Dear Child Needing Courage,

I'm glad you came to Me about this. I want you to be strong and courageous, not afraid or terrified by anything or anyone. I'll go with you wherever you go. I will never leave you or forsake you. I'll say it again: I'm out in front of you, going before you. I will never fail you, so you don't have to be afraid or discouraged. You don't need to fear disgrace or be afraid of humiliation.

I have rescued you, called your name, and made you Mine. Whether you're walking through waters or crossing rivers, you won't drown. Even when you face a firestorm, you'll remain unharmed. I'll make you strong and will help you through every trial. I will support and rescue you with My right hand. I'll grasp your hand, so you don't need to be afraid. Remember, I have not given you a spirit of timidity, but a spirit of power, love, and self-discipline.

Your Caring Father in Heaven

from Joshua 1:9; Deuteronomy 31:6, 8; Isaiah 54:4; 43:1–3; 41:10–13; 2 Timothy 1:7

Give Me Courage
GOD'S WORD OF PROMISE

FEAR NOT, for I have redeemed you;
I have summoned you by name; you
are mine. When you pass through the
waters, I will be with you; and when
you pass through the rivers, they will
not sweep over you. When you walk
through the fire, you will not be
burned; the flames will not set you
ablaze. For I am the LORD, your God,
the Holy One of Israel, your Savior.

ISAIAH 43:1–3

BE STRONG AND COURAGEOUS. DO NOT BE TERRIFIED; DO NOT BE DISCOURAGED, FOR THE LORD YOUR GOD WILL BE WITH YOU WHEREVER YOU GO.

JOSHUA 1:9

Do not fear, for I am with you; do not be dismayed, for I am your God. I will strengthen you and help you; I will uphold you with my righteous right hand.

ISAIAH 41:10

The LORD himself goes before you and will be with you; he will never leave you nor forsake you. Do not be afraid; do not be discouraged.

DEUTERONOMY 31:8

God did not give us a spirit of timidity, but a spirit of power, of love and of self-discipline.

2 TIMOTHY 1:7

Courage is
resistance to fear,
mastery of fear—
not absence of fear.

MARK TWAIN

A Graduate's Prayer

Dear Father in Heaven,

I'm eagerly writing to You about something I want to grow in and have a deeper understanding of. To me, love is the ultimate wonder, yet it is also the most confounding mystery of all. There are times when I seem to excel in even the deepest forms of love. At those times I am the person I believe I can be. Then there are the times when my selfishness barges through the door of my heart like an unwanted intruder and I can't seem to muster even the smallest affection for others. My vision narrows, and I look at others with criticism rather than concern, cool suspicion rather than trust. I long to love as You do.

You love completely and compassionately. You love the failure as well as the fulfilled, the faint as well as the forceful, the frail as well as the strong. You love me not only when I'm overflowing with love but also when I'm selfish and small. I want Your words of warmth and wisdom and promise to fill me every day and in every way so that Your love lives in me and is felt by all those I encounter. Help me to love as You do, and make me more consistently the person You've created me to be.

Your Loving Child

A Heavenly Promise

Dear Beloved Child,

The magnitude of true love can be confounding because it surpasses human knowledge. I want you to grasp hold of My love—how wide and long, how high and deep it is. The whole reason you're able to love is because I first loved you.

Now, you must love others just as I have loved you. When you do, you'll be patient and kind. You won't be jealous or boastful or proud. You won't be rude, selfish, or short-tempered. You won't keep a tally of others' failures. Your heart will find no pleasure in evil; instead, you'll enjoy truth. You'll always trust, always hope, and always remain strong.

When you are able to live a life of love, you will be filled with all of My fullness. For you see, I am love, and when you love Me and I live in you, you will live a life of love.

Your Loving Father

from Ephesians 3:17–19; 1 John 4:16, 19; 1 Corinthians 13:4–7

Help Me to Live a Life of Love
GOD'S WORD OF PROMISE

YOUR LOVE, O LORD, reaches to
the heavens, your faithfulness to the
skies….How priceless is your unfailing
love! Both high and low among men
find refuge in the shadow of your
wings. They feast on the abundance of
your house; you give them drink from
your river of delights. For with you is
the fountain of life; in your light we
see light.

PSALM 36:5, 7–9

WE LOVE BECAUSE HE
FIRST LOVED US.
1 JOHN 4:19

I pray that you, being rooted and established in love, may have power, together with all the saints, to grasp how wide and long and high and deep is the love of Christ, and to know this love that surpasses knowledge—that you may be filled to the measure of all the fullness of God.

EPHESIANS 3:17–19

LOVE IS PATIENT, LOVE IS KIND. IT DOES NOT ENVY, IT DOES NOT BOAST, IT IS NOT PROUD. IT IS NOT RUDE, IT IS NOT SELF-SEEKING, IT IS NOT EASILY ANGERED, IT KEEPS NO RECORD OF WRONGS. LOVE DOES NOT DELIGHT IN EVIL BUT REJOICES WITH THE TRUTH. IT ALWAYS PROTECTS, ALWAYS TRUSTS, ALWAYS HOPES, ALWAYS PERSEVERES.

1 CORINTHIANS 13:4–7

God is love. Whoever lives in love lives in God, and God in him.

1 JOHN 4:16

A mission of love
can come only from
union with God.

MOTHER TERESA

A Graduate's Prayer

Dear Father,

Today I need the promise of Your strength. I've looked ahead at my near future—at what will take a heavenly strength and a heart of commitment I'm not sure I possess. I already feel the temptation to compromise on some of my convictions and to lower standards that I know must be held high.

It's not a question of Your power. I know that Your superior strength has stood the tests of time and trial. Your unwavering commitment and love for me has been tested by my doubt and defiance, and not once have You failed to deliver a gentle touch or firm discipline when needed. Your patience has been stretched by my disobedience and deception, and it has always covered every corner of my life with mercy. No, it certainly isn't Your strength that I question; it's mine. I don't want my frailties to cause me to fail You in the heat of daily battles. I'm turning to You—please give me Your strength—for today, tomorrow, and forever.

Your Devoted Child

A Heavenly Promise

Dear Devoted One,

You're right to come to Me when you need strength. Hear My teachings and take them into your heart. I am your protection and your strength. I will always help you when times of trouble come. You can say to yourself, "The Lord all powerful is with me, and He is my defender."

I'll give you strength when you're tempted and power when you're weak. When you trust in Me, you will be strong. In fact, you'll rise up like a soaring eagle, run without needing to rest, and walk without growing tired.

Your struggle isn't with this world but with the unseen forces of evil; so wear My words like armor. Stand your ground using My truth as a belt and My righteousness as protection for your heart. Wear My good news of peace on your feet for readiness and speed. With your shield of faith, you can douse the flaming arrows that will be thrown at you. Protect your mind with My promised salvation, and always keep your sword of the Spirit, which is My Word. One more thing you should do and never quit doing is exactly what you've just done—pray.

Your Father Who Strengthens You

from I Chronicles 16:11; Psalms 18:32, 35; 46:1, 11;
Isaiah 40:29, 31; Ephesians 6:10–18

I Need Your Strength to Make It
GOD'S WORD OF PROMISE

BE STRONG IN THE LORD and
in his mighty power. Put on the full
armor of God so that you can take
your stand against the devil's schemes.
For our struggle is not against flesh
and blood, but against the rulers,
against the authorities, against the
powers of this dark world and against
the spiritual forces of evil in the heavenly realms.

EPHESIANS 6:10–12

It is God who arms me with strength and makes my way perfect.... You give me your shield of victory, and your right hand sustains me.

PSALM 18:32, 35

GOD IS OUR REFUGE AND STRENGTH, AN EVER-PRESENT HELP IN TROUBLE.... THE LORD ALMIGHTY IS WITH US; THE GOD OF JACOB IS OUR FORTRESS.

PSALM 46:1, 11

THE LORD IS MY STRENGTH AND MY SHIELD; MY HEART TRUSTS IN HIM, AND I AM HELPED. MY HEART LEAPS FOR JOY AND I WILL GIVE THANKS TO HIM IN SONG.

PSALM 28:7

Those who hope in the LORD will renew their strength. They will soar on wings like eagles; they will run and not grow weary, they will walk and not be faint.

ISAIAH 40:31

Look to the LORD and his strength; seek his face always.

1 CHRONICLES 16:11

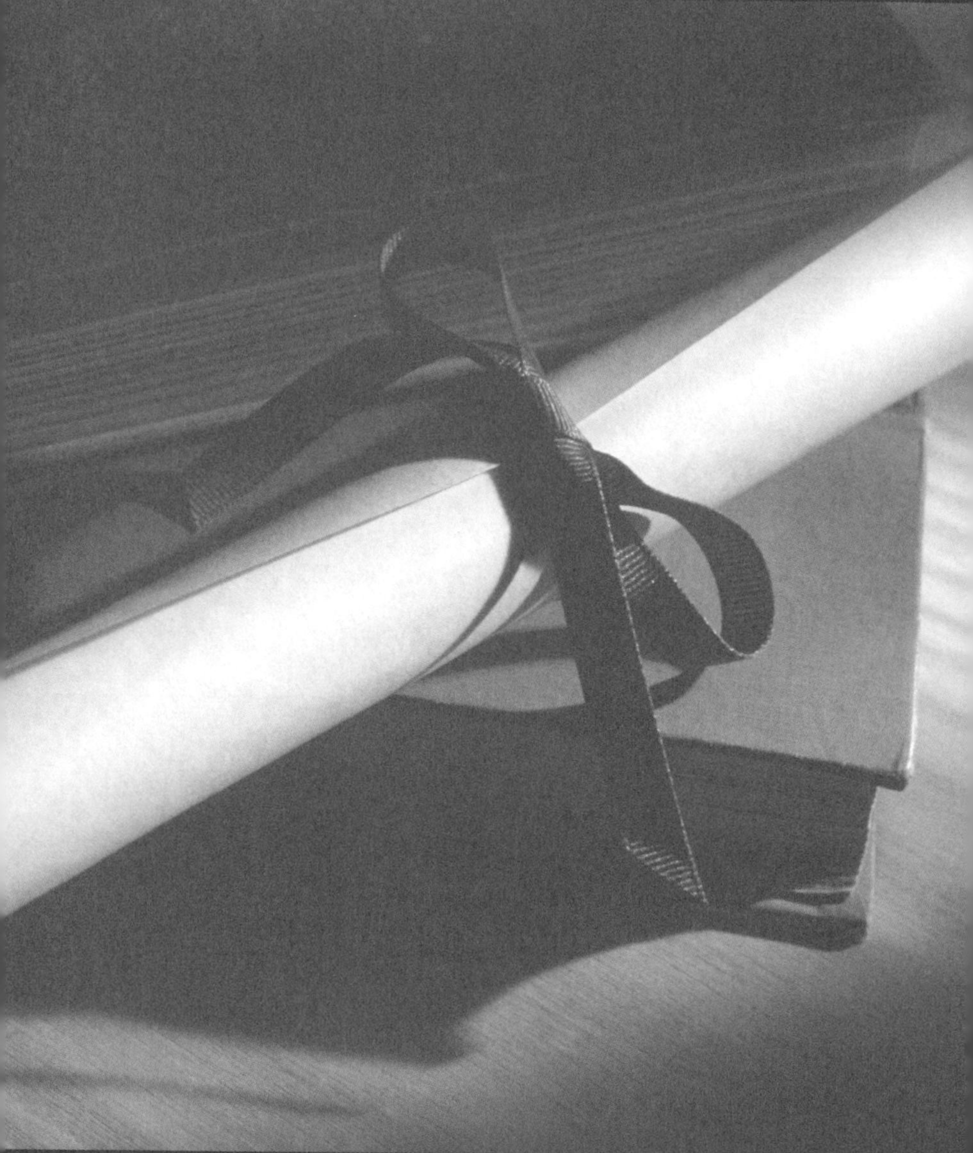

The weaker we feel,
the harder we lean on God.
And the harder we lean,
the stronger we grow.

JONI EARECKSON TADA

A Graduate's Prayer

Dear God of Patience,

I'm so glad You're patient, and right now I wish I were too. My impatience has deeply affected my family—the very people I ought to have the most patience with. When something doesn't go smoothly, I become entirely too short-tempered and short-sighted. I've even become irritable with my friends. I care about these people, but You wouldn't know it by the way I've been behaving toward them.

The worst part of all is that I have grown impatient with You. I'm ashamed to say it, but it's true. There are certain things in my life and about myself that I want to see changed. I've prayed hard about them, but everything remains the same. I want my life to change yesterday, not tomorrow or sometime in the distant future! I want my problems to go away immediately and to take my weaknesses with them.

But right now, I'm simply praying for patience. Not just normal, everyday patience—I need the heavenly kind. The kind that shows that I love my family and friends. The kind that allows me to make mistakes and grants me time to transform my character flaws. I especially desire the kind that waits on You with total trust and confidence.

Your Impatient Child

A Heavenly Promise

Dear Impatient Child,

You've been thinking about your trials and tensions all wrong. You should regard them with joy because you know that these very troubles are what will result in your gaining the patience you desire. Then this patience will produce the character you hope to have; in turn, that character produces more hope—a hope that never disappoints because I've poured out My love until it fills your heart. Consider the example of the farmer who waits patiently on the land until it gives him a crop; note how patient he is in waiting for the rain to come.

As you are waiting, you should always pray and not give up. When you call out for Me and come to Me and pray, you can be sure that I will listen. Call on Me when you're in trouble. I will help you, and you will bring Me honor. Don't become discouraged in doing good things, for you can be sure that they'll produce fruit at just the right time. Grasp hold of the hope that you talk about and never let go, knowing what I have promised and that I am faithful.

Your Patient Father

from James 1:2–4; Romans 5:3; James 5:7–8; Luke 18:1; Jeremiah 29:12; Galatians 6:9

Help Me to Be Patient
GOD'S WORD OF PROMISE

Consider it PURE JOY, my brothers, whenever you face trials of many kinds, because you know that the testing of your faith develops perseverance. Perseverance must finish its work so that you may be mature and complete, not lacking anything.

JAMES 1:2–4

WE ALSO REJOICE IN OUR SUFFERINGS, BECAUSE WE
KNOW THAT SUFFERING PRODUCES PERSEVERANCE;
PERSEVERANCE, CHARACTER; AND CHARACTER, HOPE.

ROMANS 5:3–4

Persevere so that when you
have done the will of God,
you will receive what he
has promised.

HEBREWS 10:36

Jesus told his disciples
a parable to show them
that they should always
pray and not give up.

LUKE 18:1

LET US NOT BECOME WEARY IN DOING
GOOD, FOR AT THE PROPER TIME WE WILL
REAP A HARVEST IF WE DO NOT GIVE UP.

GALATIANS 6:9

Be patient
and stand
firm, because
the Lord's
coming is
near.

JAMES 5:8

ompleted a Course of

Education in this School,

tion of Colleges and Schools

a graduate of this School

Diploma

No one will ever know
the full depth of his capacity
for patience and humility
as long as nothing bothers him.
It is only when times are troubled
and difficult that he can see
how much of either is in him.

SAINT FRANCIS OF ASSISI

A Graduate's Prayer

Dear God of Guidance,

I've been making plans lately and writing down goals: things I would very much like to achieve and places I want to go. Then it struck me. Can I get there by myself? Can I define my desires, pursue my plans, or reach my destinations without Your guidance? Is it possible for me to reach the peaks, sit on the summits, or climb the steep and cavernous walls of life without Your direction? I answered my own questions with a resounding no.

I can't even predict what will happen tomorrow, so how can I map out the course of my life?

I'm sure there are dangers ahead that I can't detect and storms I can't forecast. That's what brings me to You. I need to feel Your strong hand grasping mine so that when I stumble, I won't fall. Lead me with steps that won't be too large, to destinations not too far for me to reach, and to depths I can't yet even dream of. You know me better than I know myself. You know what I'm capable of. You also know which mountains I'm too weak to climb, which problems I'm too blind to see, and which weaknesses I'm too proud to admit. I can't reach my destination on my own. I will not proceed without You. I'll wait for You to lead me.

Your Faithful Follower

A Heavenly Promise

Dear Faithful Follower,

It's true that people make many plans, but you know that only I can make them a reality. When you rely on Me in whatever you do, your plans will succeed. When people say, "Today or tomorrow we'll go here, build a business, and make lots of money," they don't know what they're saying. They don't even know what will happen tomorrow. Listen for My voice. Whether you go right or left, you will hear Me saying, "This is the way; walk in it."

I will constantly lead you and will supply your needs in barren times. You'll be like a garden that's always being watered and like a spring that never runs dry. In everything you do, simply recognize Me, and I will make sure the road you're on is straight. I'm committed to instructing you and teaching you which way you should go. I will advise you and protect you. I'll turn darkness into light right in front of you and will make rough places smooth. These are the things I will do, and I will not fail you.

Your Guiding Father

from Proverbs 16:1, 3; James 4:13–14; Isaiah 30:21; 58:11; Proverbs 3:6; Psalm 32:8; Isaiah 42:16

You Lead; I'll Follow
GOD'S WORD OF PROMISE

I WILL LEAD the blind by ways they have not known, along unfamiliar paths I will guide them; I will turn the darkness into light before them and make the rough places smooth. These are the things I will do; I will not forsake them.

ISAIAH 42:16

To man belong the plans of the heart, but from the LORD comes the reply of the tongue.... Commit to the LORD whatever you do, and your plans will succeed.

PROVERBS 16:1, 3

The LORD will guide you always; he will satisfy your needs in a sun-scorched land and will strengthen your frame. You will be like a well-watered garden, like a spring whose waters never fail.

ISAIAH 58:11

WHETHER YOU TURN TO THE RIGHT OR TO THE LEFT, YOUR EARS WILL HEAR A VOICE BEHIND YOU, SAYING, "THIS IS THE WAY; WALK IN IT."

ISAIAH 30:21

I will instruct you and teach you in the way you should go; I will counsel you and watch over you.

PSALM 32:8

Before us is a future all unknown,
a path untrod;
Beside us is a friend well loved
and known—
That friend is God.

ANONYMOUS

ANONYMOUS

A Graduate's Prayer

Dearly Loved Father,

What I'm writing to You about is extremely important to me. In fact, nothing could be more crucial to my future than this one thing. I want to accomplish many things in life, and I've carefully crafted plans to help me achieve my goals. However, I'm aware that nothing I can dream, design, or devise will be accomplished or completed if You don't give it Your blessing.

I'm just one small person in a huge world; yet You seem to take a special interest in doing the magnificent with the mediocre and the sensational with the simple. You've anointed people who were considered insignificant and set them on thrones; You've made the smallest of nations mighty and power-ful. You've even strengthened armies locked in battles that seemed all but lost, turning defeat into triumph.

I'm asking for Your blessing on my hopes and dreams and on each step I take to accomplish what is set before me. Bless me when I work and when I rest, when I run and when I walk, when I get discouraged and when I feel indestructible. With Your blessing, I can begin my march toward tomorrow.

Your Blessed Child

A Heavenly Promise

Dear Blessed Child,

You've made many plans and charted your course, but never forget that I am the one who determines your steps. In everything you do, acknowledge who I am, and I'll make your paths straight. When I delight in where you're going, you can be sure that I will make your steps firm. I will give countless blessings when you trust in Me. I'll send a rainstorm of blessings!

Delight yourself in Me, and I'll grant you the desires of your heart. Entrust your future, your hopes and dreams to Me, and this is what I will do: I will make your life shine like the dawn and your plans and purposes like the afternoon sun. I know the plans I have for you, plans to prosper you and not to bring you harm, plans to confirm your hope and future. These blessings will fall on you and follow you if you obey Me. You'll be blessed whether you're in the city or in the country. You'll be blessed when you're coming in and going out. I am with you and will save you; I will rejoice over you, and you will rest in My love.

Your God of Blessing

from Proverbs 16:9; 3:6; Psalm 37:23; Romans 10:12; Ezekiel 34:26; Psalm 37:4–6; Jeremiah 29:11; Deuteronomy 28:2–3, 6

I Can't Go On
without Your Blessing
GOD'S WORD OF PROMISE

THE LORD had said to Abram,
"Leave your country, your people and
your father's household and go to the
land I will show you. I will make you
into a great nation and I will bless you;
I will make your name great, and you
will be a blessing. I will bless those
who bless you."

GENESIS 12:1–3

I WILL BLESS THEM....
I WILL SEND DOWN
SHOWERS IN SEASON;
THERE WILL BE SHOWERS
OF BLESSING.
EZEKIEL 34:26

"I know the plans I have for you," declares the LORD, "plans to prosper you and not to harm you, plans to give you hope and a future."
JEREMIAH 29:11

Blessings will come upon you and accompany you if you obey the LORD your God.
DEUTERONOMY 28:2

IN HIS HEART A MAN PLANS HIS COURSE, BUT THE LORD DETERMINES HIS STEPS.
PROVERBS 16:9

If the LORD delights in a man's way, he makes his steps firm.
PSALM 37:23

Never undertake anything
for which you wouldn't
have the courage to ask
the blessings of heaven.

GEORG CHRISTOPH LICHTENBERG

A Graduate's Prayer

Dear Father of Power,

I've been examining my life, and it has led me to request something spectacular from You. I want to experience more of Your awesome power in every aspect of my life.

I'm amazed by Your power as seen every day in the grandeur of Your creation. I'm moved by the magnificence of Your artistry. Everything from the stunning peaks of the tallest mountains to the mysterious depths of the vast oceans bears Your signature of power. When storms rage, winds blow, and lightning streaks across the sky; these are evidences of Your thunderous voice heralding Your living power. Your power is expressed in the energy of Your golden dawns and in the peace of Your rich, brilliant sunsets.

Just as You reveal Your power in these works of creation, so I want You to reveal Your power in my life. I want all that I do and all that I am to bear Your signature of power. I want my actions to be so bright that they light up the horizons. I want my words to resound with thunderous truth. My greatest desire is that my life would be a portrait of Your power, painted by Your almighty hand.

Your Humble Child

A Heavenly Promise

Dear Humble Child,

My answer comes from heaven with the power of My right hand. Counsel and judgment are Mine; I have understanding and power. By Me kings reign and rulers pass laws; by Me princes govern and nobles lead on earth. With Me are riches and honor, enduring wealth and prosperity. My works are better than the purest gold and surpass the finest silver. Who has measured the waters in his hand, or with his hand marked off the heavens? Who has held the earth's dust in a basket or placed the mountains on a scale and the hills on a balance? To whom will you compare Me? Who is My equal?

I display the stars one by one and call them by name. Because of My great power and strength, not one of them is missing. I will empower you. For I am a light and a shield, and I give you benefits and honor. I have given you a spirit of power, of love, and of self-discipline.

Your Powerful and Devoted Father

from Psalm 20:6; Proverbs 8:14–16, 18–19;
Isaiah 40:12, 25–26, 29, 31; Psalm 84:11–12; 2 Timothy 1:7

I Need a Power Greater than My Own

"To whom WILL YOU COMPARE me? Or who is my equal?" says the Holy One. Lift your eyes and look to the heavens: Who created all these? He who brings out the starry host one by one, and calls them each by name. Because of his great power and mighty strength, not one of them is missing.

ISAIAH 40:25–26

The name of the LORD is a strong tower;
the righteous run to it and are safe.

PROVERBS 18:10

GREAT IS OUR
LORD AND
MIGHTY IN
POWER....THE
LORD SUSTAINS
THE HUMBLE.
PSALM 147:5–6

The LORD saves his
anointed; he answers
him from his holy
heaven with the
saving power of
his right hand.

PSALM 20:6

YOU, DEAR CHILDREN,
ARE FROM GOD....THE
ONE WHO IS IN YOU
IS GREATER THAN
THE ONE WHO IS
IN THE WORLD.
1 JOHN 4:4

He gives strength to the
weary and increases the
power of the weak.

ISAIAH 40:29

I am only one, but I am one.
I cannot do everything,
but I can do something.
And that which I do,
by the grace of God,
I will do.

DWIGHT L. MOODY

DWIGHT L.
MOODY

A Graduate's Prayer

Dear God,

I'm feeling a mysterious kind of loneliness. I know the answer should be obvious: go to church, get with friends, and stay close to my family. I've done all that, yet I'm still troubled by this uneasy isolation. As my life takes a different path than many of my friends and as I set out for the first time on my own, I wonder who will care what I face every day—what frustrates me, fuels my anger, or feeds my soul. Who will be there to share my heartaches, hassles, celebrations, and triumphs?

I want to be independent, but I don't really want to feel isolated—alone in the world. I hunger for relationships in which both parties hold the other up, share one another's sadness, and cheer each victory. I want forgiveness to be plentiful, failures to find understanding, and needs to be met.

I want to develop new relationships that will fulfill these needs, but I also want to feel closer to You, because only in Your presence can all of my heart's desires be fulfilled. I need and want Your presence in my life. Especially now, with the swirl of changes and new beginnings in my life, I want to draw closer and be reassured that You'll always be with me—that You'll never leave me alone.

Your Devoted Child

A Heavenly Promise

Dear Child,

I'm not distant from you. Come near to Me, and I'll come near to you. When you call, I will answer; when you cry for help, I'll respond by saying, "Here I am." You are precious in My eyes, and I truly love you. I'll never leave you. I am a Father to you, and you are My child. I'm with you wherever you go.

Love Me with all of your heart, and love your friends and family as much as you love yourself. You can't do anything more important than this. That love must be the most sincere kind that hates evil and holds tightly to what is good. Be devoted to others with a brotherly love. Honor and admire others above yourself. Never let your enthusiasm fade away, but keep your intensity burning in support of Me.

Delight yourself with hope; be patient even when you're wounded, and be unwavering in your prayer life. Do everything necessary to maintain unity in the Spirit. Put up with others, and forgive whatever you may be holding against them. Forgive, just like I've forgiven you, and I'll be with you until the end of time.

Your God Who Is Always Near

from James 4:8; Isaiah 58:9; 43:4; Deuteronomy 31:6;
2 Corinthians 6:18; Genesis 28:15; Mark 12:29–31; Romans 12:9–12;
Ephesians 4:3; Matthew 28:20

Your Presence Is Requested
GOD'S WORD OF PROMISE

IF...YOU SEEK THE LORD your
God, you will find him if you look
for him with all your heart and with
all your soul....For the LORD your
God is a merciful God; he will not
abandon or destroy you or forget the
covenant with your forefathers, which
he confirmed to them by oath.

DEUTERONOMY 4:29, 31

THE LORD YOUR GOD GOES WITH YOU; HE WILL NEVER LEAVE YOU NOR FORSAKE YOU.

DEUTERONOMY 31:6

I am with you and will watch over you wherever you go.

GENESIS 28:15

You will call, and the LORD will answer; you will cry for help, and he will say: Here am I.

ISAIAH 58:9

I AM WITH YOU ALWAYS, TO THE VERY END OF THE AGE.

MATTHEW 28:20

Come near to God and he will come near to you.

JAMES 4:8

"I will be a Father to you, and you will be my sons and daughters," says the Lord Almighty.

2 CORINTHIANS 6:18

Human fellowship can
go to great lengths,
but not all the way.
Fellowship with God
can go to all lengths.

OSWALD CHAMBERS

A Graduate's Prayer

Dear God,

What will happen to my plans for the future? They seem right to me, but how can I know? Others are convinced I should go a different direction. I'm writing this with a little fear, a bit of confusion, and a lot of anxiety. I felt certain about my plans, certain You would bless them. I was sure that You would walk with me down the path and help me win the prize I'm pursuing. But now I'm feeling less confident.

Now I'm questioning my dreams, doubting my path. You can see things I don't; is there a danger in my plans that might damage my life? Is there pain or loss I could not withstand? Are there cracks in the foundation of my future that would collapse the walls around me? Or should I hold steady and follow the course I felt You had laid out before me?

I need to know because I believed in the dreams; but the obstacles and the doubts of others haunt me. I fear daring to dream. I don't want to take the wrong path. You are my hope and future. I long to hear Your answer.

Your Uncertain Child

A Heavenly Promise

Dear Uncertain Child,

I want you to trust Me with all your heart and not depend on your own understanding. Acknowledge Me in everything you do, and I'll make certain that your path is straight. Find your fulfillment in Me, and I'll give you what your heart desires. Continue to surrender your plans to Me and trust Me, and I will do it. You must understand that you might choose a way that seems absolutely right to you but will end in destruction.

I will keep you from getting badly hurt, and I'll watch over your whole life. I'll keep a close eye on everything you do all the days of your life. Hear My words: My thinking about things is different from your thinking. Your ways are not the same as Mine. My thinking and ways are as far from yours as the earth is from the sky. Even when you have disappointment, you will be happy because I'll comfort you. When you hunger to do right more than anything else, you'll be happy because I will completely satisfy you. I am your sun and shield; I give favor and honor; there is not one good thing that I will keep from you when you walk blamelessly. Those who trust in Me will be blessed.

Your God of Grace

from Proverbs 3:5–6; Psalm 37:4–5; Proverbs 14:12; Psalm 121:7–8; Isaiah 55:8–9; Matthew 5:4, 6; Psalm 84:11–12

Which Path Should I Take?
GOD'S WORD OF PROMISE

DELIGHT YOURSELF in the LORD
and he will give you the desires of your
heart. Commit your way to the LORD;
trust in him and he will do this: He
will make your righteousness shine like
the dawn, the justice of your cause like
the noonday sun.

PSALM 37:4–6

THE LORD BESTOWS FAVOR AND HONOR; NO GOOD THING DOES HE WITHHOLD FROM THOSE WHOSE WALK IS BLAMELESS.

PSALM 84:11

Trust in the LORD with all your heart and lean not on your own understanding; in all your ways acknowledge him, and he will make your paths straight.

PROVERBS 3:5–6

"My thoughts are not your thoughts, neither are your ways my ways," declares the LORD. "As the heavens are higher than the earth, so are my ways higher than your ways and my thoughts than your thoughts."

ISAIAH 55:8–9

The LORD will keep you from all harm— he will watch over your life; the LORD will watch over your coming and going both now and forevermore.

PSALM 121:7–8

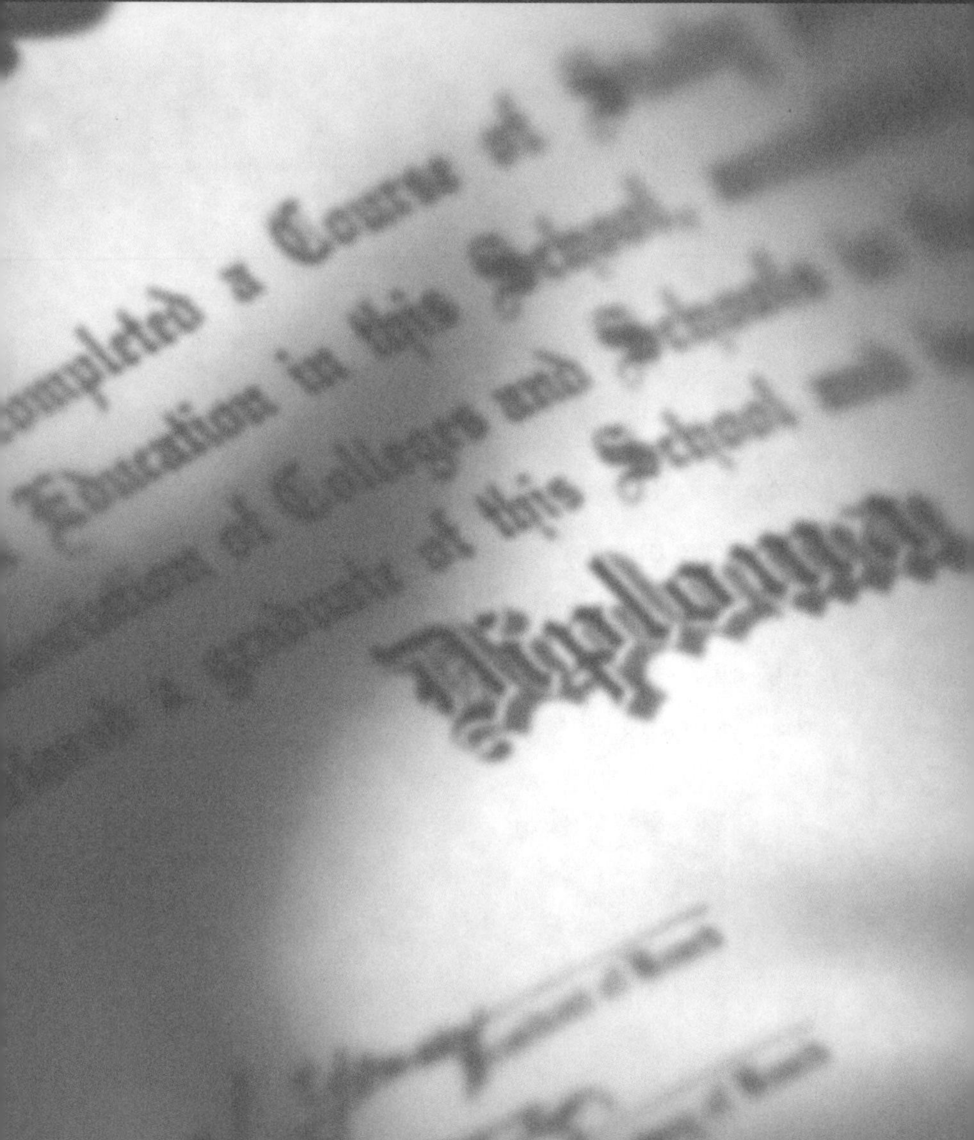

God is gracious in providing
not only the plan,
but also the Spirit
as our leader and guide.
When indeed, the line is fine,
God is our divine balancing pole.

WAYNE WATSON

A Graduate's Prayer

Dear Father,

You just can't imagine the things I hear every day. Advertisements bombard me, promising that if I take a certain pill, purchase a certain kind of clothing, or drive the right car, I'll be successful and happy. If I go on the right diet or purchase a piece of exercise equipment, I'll have the physique I've always dreamed of. Day after day, more and more is promised, and less and less is actually believable. It has begun to impact how I see, hear, and speak to everyone I come in contact with.

My soul hungers for authenticity. It hungers for real, relevant words that can be counted on as truth instead of the endless smoke screen of sentences that fog my world every day—truth that actually changes things from what they are into what I believe they could be.

Who can I believe? What is really right? And where do I find answers that will do more than disappoint me and betray my trust? You are the One I turn to for truth. Through Your words I know I'll find a reason to believe like a child again. Pour out Your promises on me and into my eager heart.

Your Child in Search of Truth

A Heavenly Promise

Dear Searching Child,

My words are perfect, and they give new strength. The rules I've written can be trusted, and they make ordinary people wise. My decisions are true and completely right. My Word is a lamp to your feet that lights up the path you walk. My Word is alive and active. It's sharper than any double-edged sword; it penetrates even between the soul and spirit, the joints and bones. It evaluates what you think and the attitudes of your heart.

Love My teachings! Think about them all day long. My words are true from the start, and you'll find that My rules for living are fair forever. You'll be blessed when you read them and blessed when you let them soak into your heart. All Scripture is from My mouth and is useful for teaching, disciplining, correcting, and training, so that you are completely prepared to perform every good work. My Word is certain, and you'll do well to pay attention to it, as though it were a light shining in a dark place until the day breaks and the morning star rises in your heart.

Your Father of Truth

from Psalms 19:7–9; 119:105; Hebrews 4:12; Psalm 119:97, 160; Revelation 1:3; 2 Timothy 3:16–17; 2 Peter 1:19

Who Can I Believe?
GOD'S WORD OF PROMISE

The law of THE LORD IS PERFECT, reviving the soul. The statutes of the LORD are trustworthy, making wise the simple. The precepts of the LORD are right, giving joy to the heart. The commands of the LORD are radiant, giving light to the eyes. The fear of the LORD is pure, enduring forever. The ordinances of the LORD are sure and altogether righteous.

PSALM 19:7–9

All Scripture is God-breathed and is useful for teaching, rebuking, correcting and training in righteousness, so that the man of God may be thoroughly equipped for every good work.

2 TIMOTHY 3:16–17

OH, HOW I LOVE YOUR LAW! I MEDITATE ON IT ALL DAY LONG....ALL YOUR WORDS ARE TRUE; ALL YOUR RIGHTEOUS LAWS ARE ETERNAL.

PSALM 119:97, 160

The word of God is living and active....It penetrates even to dividing soul and spirit, joints and marrow.

HEBREWS 4:12

We have the word of the prophets made more certain, and you will do well to pay attention to it, as to a light shining in a dark place.

2 PETER 1:19

Your word is a lamp to my feet and a light for my path.

PSALM 119:105

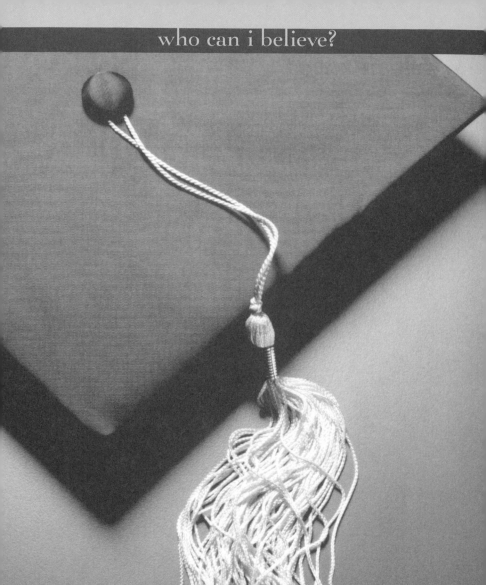

Rather than love,
than money,
than fame,
give me truth.

HENRY DAVID THOREAU

HENRY DAVID
THOREAU

A Graduate's Prayer

Dear God and Father,

Something is really bothering me, and I know I'll find the answers I need from You. I'm feeling overwhelming anxiety. It's not just one particular thing. My mind jumps from one anxious thought to another. I find myself concerned about money. Will I have enough to do the things I really want to do? Will I be able to make it on my own? Then I start worrying about my life. Am I making the right choices about my future? Am I taking the right path in my education and career? Will I be successful? Will I be happy? Will I accomplish anything worth mentioning, or will I simply exist and never really amount to much?

I watch the news and start worrying for the first time about serious things, like the economy and the job market, the ethics and morality of our country, and the fragile peace that exists— or too often is shattered—in the world.

I know You don't want me to be consumed with such anxious thoughts. I know You're not worried about the future. You've seen the beginning and end and know how everything will work out. You hold tomorrow in Your hands. Help me to find assurance and confidence in Your power. Bring to me Your peace through Your promises.

Your Anxious Child

A Heavenly Promise

Dear Anxious Child,

Just give all your worries to Me, because I care deeply for you. Don't be anxious about anything, but in everything, with a thankful heart, bring your prayers and requests to Me. My peace, which goes well beyond all human understanding, will protect your heart and mind in Christ. I will meet all your needs according to My own glorious wealth. I give authentic peace to those who depend on Me because they trust Me. You can always trust Me; I am your rock forever.

I'm telling you not to worry about your life, what you'll eat or drink, or about your body, what you'll wear. Isn't life more important than the food you eat or the clothes you wear? You will be like a tree with roots planted by the stream. It doesn't fear when heat comes, and its leaves are always green. It doesn't worry even in a drought, and it never fails to bear fruit.

So don't let tomorrow trouble you. You can be confident that in all matters, I'll work things out for your good because I love you and because you've been called to fulfill My purpose for you.

Your Assuring God

from 1 Peter 5:7; Philippians 4:6–7, 19; Isaiah 26:3–4; Matthew 6:25; Jeremiah 17:8; Matthew 6:34; Romans 8:28

I'm Anxious about the Future
GOD'S WORD OF PROMISE

DO NOT BE ANXIOUS about anything, but in everything, by prayer and petition, with thanksgiving, present your requests to God. And the peace of God, which transcends all understanding, will guard your hearts and your minds in Christ Jesus.

PHILIPPIANS 4:6–7

GOD WILL MEET ALL YOUR NEEDS ACCORDING
TO HIS GLORIOUS RICHES IN CHRIST JESUS.
PHILIPPIANS 4:19

You will keep in perfect peace him whose
mind is steadfast, because he trusts in you.
ISAIAH 26:3

In all things

God works for

the good of

those who love

him, who have

been called

according to

his purpose.

ROMANS 8:28

DO NOT WORRY ABOUT
TOMORROW, FOR TOMORROW
WILL WORRY ABOUT ITSELF.
MATTHEW 6:34

Cast all your anxiety on him
because he cares for you.
1 PETER 5:7

67

Anxiety does not empty tomorrow
of its sorrows
but only empties today
of its strength.

<small>CHARLES HADDON SPURGEON</small>

A Graduate's Prayer

Dear Father and Helper,

People tell me these are the best years of my life. They haven't been in school lately. Can they know the fear of wondering if the seething kids in the corner might one day show up with automatic weapons? Could they fathom the number of my peers who have suffered physical, mental, or sexual abuse? Do they have any idea how many hopeless, hurting young people have contemplated—or attempted—suicide? Could they possibly relate to the devastating loneliness and isolation that drives students to engage in anything—drinking, drugs, sex—that might bring acceptance or popularity, or at least dull the pain?

My world can be a dangerous place full of temptations, pressures, and problems. And now I'm launching out into a world that's even bigger, more difficult, and sometimes more dangerous. It's too big to handle on my own. But I don't have to.

You've always offered help in my troubles. Your torch of truth has been a constant source of light shining in the darkness. Thank You for carrying me on Your shoulders through life's storms and shielding me from the wind and the rains that hammered against me. I raise my hands and heart in thanksgiving for Your help in my times of trouble. Thank You.

Your Trusting Child

A Heavenly Promise

Dear Trusting Child,

Consider Me a safe place where you can hide, and I will protect you from trouble and surround you with My songs of deliverance. I am your shepherd who will not leave you in need. I will help you lie down in flourishing fields; I'll show you quiet waters and refresh your soul.

Even if you find yourself walking through the dark valley of death, you won't fear any evil, because I'm right there with you. You can rest assured that goodness and love will accompany you every day you live and that you'll live in My house forever. I've told you these things so you can find peace in Me. In this world you will have trouble—but here's My promise to you: I have overcome the world!

Your Protecting Father

from Psalms 32:7; 23:1–4, 6; John 16:33

You Have Been My Help
God's Word of Promise

THE LORD IS MY SHEPHERD,
I shall not be in want. He makes me
lie down in green pastures, he leads
me beside quiet waters, he restores
my soul. He guides me in paths of
righteousness....Even though I walk
through the valley of the shadow of
death, I will fear no evil, for you are
with me.

PSALM 23:1–4

I have told you these things, so that in me you may have peace. In this world you will have trouble. But take heart! I have overcome the world.

JOHN 16:33

YOU ARE MY HIDING PLACE; YOU WILL PROTECT ME FROM TROUBLE AND SURROUND ME WITH SONGS OF DELIVERANCE.

PSALM 32:7

My flesh and my heart may fail, but God is the strength of my heart and my portion forever.

PSALM 73:26

The LORD is good, a refuge in times of trouble. He cares for those who trust in him.

NAHUM 1:7

Helplessness is your best prayer.
It calls from your heart
to the heart of God
with greater effect
than all your uttered pleas.

OLE HALLESBY

A Graduate's Prayer

Dear God,

I just wanted to write and say "Thank You." You fill my life in so many ways that I'm overflowing with gratitude. It's Your strength that I depend on and seek when I face obstacles and troubles, and it always comes in steady supply. Because it's Your power in me and not my own, I can live without fear. Triumphs have replaced failures.

I'm grateful also for the guidance You give. I follow where You lead, and I feel Your strong hand on my shoulder. Life is far less a mystery because You've shared with me the truth about my days on earth and the dangers that lie in wait for me, and You've shown me where my help comes from. I find Your words, wisdom, and guidance faultless.

Even when I fail You or weaken and worry, You're patient with me, wanting me to grow into the person only You can make me. You're my protection, power, hope, and strength. My soul is filled with gratitude. Thank You for revealing to me the life I could never have lived without You.

Your Thankful Child

A Heavenly Promise

Dear Child,

My loved ones will always rest secure in Me, and those I love rest between My shoulders. Come to Me with thanksgiving and surround Me with praise; give thanks and honor to My name. My goodness and love go on forever, and I will remain faithful to you through all time. I'll strengthen you and bless you with peace. I am your light and your rescuer. You are secure because I give you hope; you can look around you and rest safely. You can lie down without being afraid, and many will want to be your friend.

Even if the mountains are shaken and the hills disappear, My unfailing love for you will not be shaken, nor will My covenant of peace be taken away. I have great compassion for you. I'm with you, and I'm strong enough to save you. You give Me great pleasure. I will quiet you with My love and sing over you with great joy. I have come so that you can have the fullest life possible.

Your Loving God

from Deuteronomy 33:12; Psalms 100:4–5; 29:11; 27:1;
Job 11:18–19; Isaiah 54:10; Zephaniah 3:17; John 10:10

I Want to Thank You
GOD'S WORD OF PROMISE

THE LORD IS GOD. It is he who made us, and we are his; we are his people, the sheep of his pasture. Enter his gates with thanksgiving and his courts with praise; give thanks to him and praise his name. For the LORD is good and his love endures forever; his faithfulness continues through all generations.

PSALM 100:3–5

"THOUGH THE MOUNTAINS BE SHAKEN AND THE HILLS BE REMOVED, YET MY UNFAILING LOVE FOR YOU WILL NOT BE SHAKEN NOR MY COVENANT OF PEACE BE REMOVED," SAYS THE LORD.

ISAIAH 54:10

Let the beloved of the LORD rest secure in him, for he shields him all day long, and the one the LORD loves rests between his shoulders.

DEUTERONOMY 33:12

I have come that they may have life, and have it to the full.

JOHN 10:10

God is to us like the sky
to a small bird,
which cannot see its outer limits
and cannot reach its
distant horizons,
but can only lose itself
in the greatness and
immensity of the blueness.

JOHN POWELL

A Graduate's Prayer

Dear God of Love,

I've figured something out, and I wanted to let You know right away. It won't be a surprise to You, but it seems I need to be reminded of it from time to time. Your love is what I need more than anything else. I told You it wouldn't be a surprise to You. And do You know what else I've discovered? I like it that way.

It's absolutely wonderful to know that when I fail—and I do quite often—I can curl up in Your reassuring embrace, be forgiven (including forgiving myself), and leave the guilt behind. When I'm wounded, Your love comes quickly to soothe the pain and quicken my healing. As I daily run the race of life, Your loving voice encourages me and urges me on to the finish line. It's great to know that because of Your devotion, I'm always considered a winner. Your love is full of the protection I need, the power I depend on, and the promise that sustains me. There's something else I wanted to tell You too. I love You.

Your Dearly Loved Child

A Heavenly Promise

Dearly Loved Child,

I have loved you with an eternal love; I have pulled you close with loving-kindness. In all things, you are more than a winner through My love. There is nothing in all creation that will separate you from My love—not death or life, not angels or demons, not the present, the future, or any other power. May you, being firmly planted and formed in love, have power, with all My children, to comprehend just how wide and long and high and deep is the love of Christ. And may you know this love that goes beyond human knowledge so that you may be filled with all My fullness.

In a race, all the runners run; but only one gets the prize. Run to win the prize. I am with you, and I'm strong enough to save. I take great pride in you. I will calm you with love and rejoice over you with singing. Remember what is written: "No eye has seen, no ear has heard, no mind has conceived what I have prepared for those who love Me."

Your Loving and Devoted God

from Jeremiah 31:3; Romans 8:37–39; Ephesians 3:17–19;
1 Corinthians 9:24; Zephaniah 3:17; 1 Corinthians 2:9

Your Love Is All I Need
GOD'S WORD OF PROMISE

WE ARE MORE than conquerors through him who loved us....Neither death nor life, neither angels nor demons, neither the present nor the future, nor any powers, neither height nor depth, nor anything else in all creation, will be able to separate us from the love of God that is in Christ Jesus our Lord.

ROMANS 8:37–39

The LORD your God is with you, he is mighty
to save. He will take great delight in you, he
will quiet you with his love, he will rejoice
over you with singing.

ZEPHANIAH 3:17

I HAVE LOVED YOU WITH AN EVERLASTING LOVE;
I HAVE DRAWN YOU WITH LOVING-KINDNESS.

JEREMIAH 31:3

I pray that you, being rooted and
established in love, may have power,
together with all the saints, to grasp
how wide and long and high and deep
is the love of Christ, and to know this
love that surpasses knowledge.

EPHESIANS 3:17–19

We know and
rely on the
love God has
for us.

1 JOHN 4:16

85

completed a Course of
Education in this School,
of College and Schools to
a schedule of this School and

Diploma

He who knows he is loved
can be content
with a piece of bread,
while all the luxuries of the world
cannot satisfy
the craving of the lonely.

FRANCES J. ROBERTS

FRANCES J.
ROBERTS

my personal graduation prayer

DATE _____

_____
_____
_____
_____
_____
_____
_____
_____
_____
_____
_____
_____
_____
_____
_____
_____
_____
_____
_____
_____
_____
_____